A Mark Dahle Portfolio

The Sea Bream

No Life Lasts Forever

(Fables About Aesop #4)

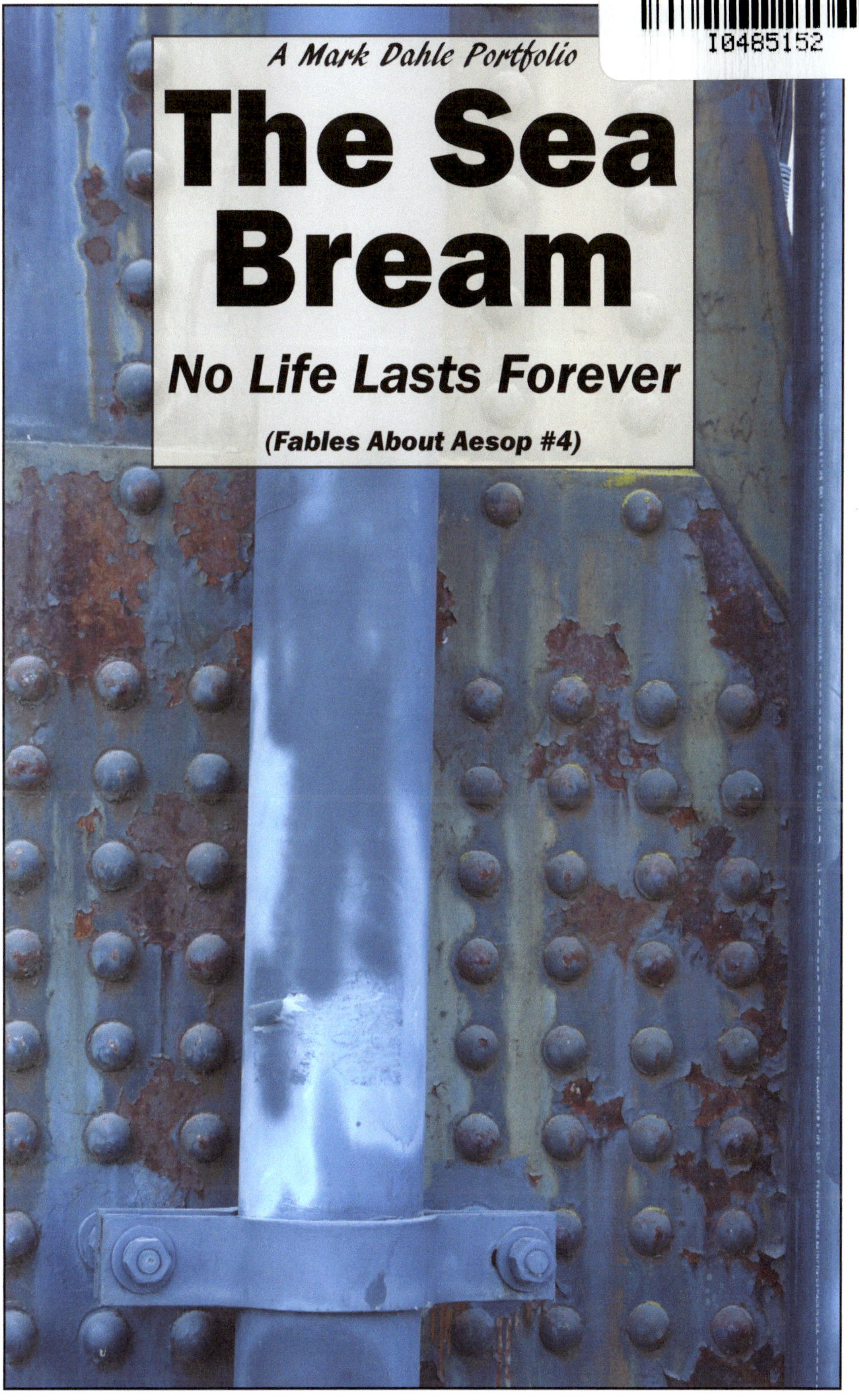

Mark Dahle has written many great fables about Aesop.
This is #4.

~ ~ ~

Mark Dahle Portfolios can be read in a few minutes and enjoyed
for a lifetime.

Unlike many picture books, the text is not related to the beautiful
painting at the right and the photographs that follow. This might
seem a little weird at first. One thing that helps is to order more
portfolios until you get used to it. In the meantime, feel free to
draw your own pictures of Aesop if you like.

This portfolio includes a photo of a brilliant 36 x 24 inch painting
(at the right), twenty-five beautiful pictures of Portland, Oregon,
and a story about Aesop's childhood.

Photographs in this book are available in very limited editions.
See http://www.MarkDahle.com for more information and for
previews of upcoming portfolios.

*We do our best to create portfolios free of editing mistakes. But it's hard to
catch everything. We reward people who report errors in any Mark Dahle
portfolio. For details see MarkDahle.com/Typos.html or send an email to
MarkDahle@aol.com with the subject line "Typos." Thanks!*

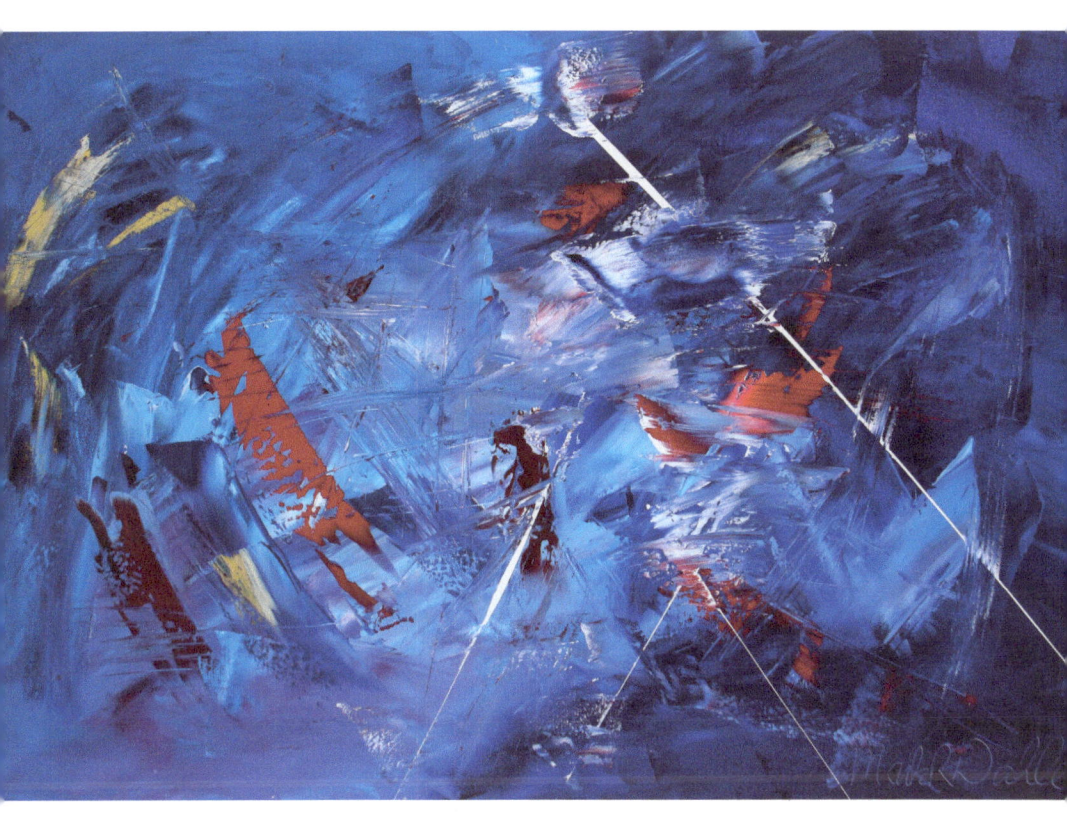

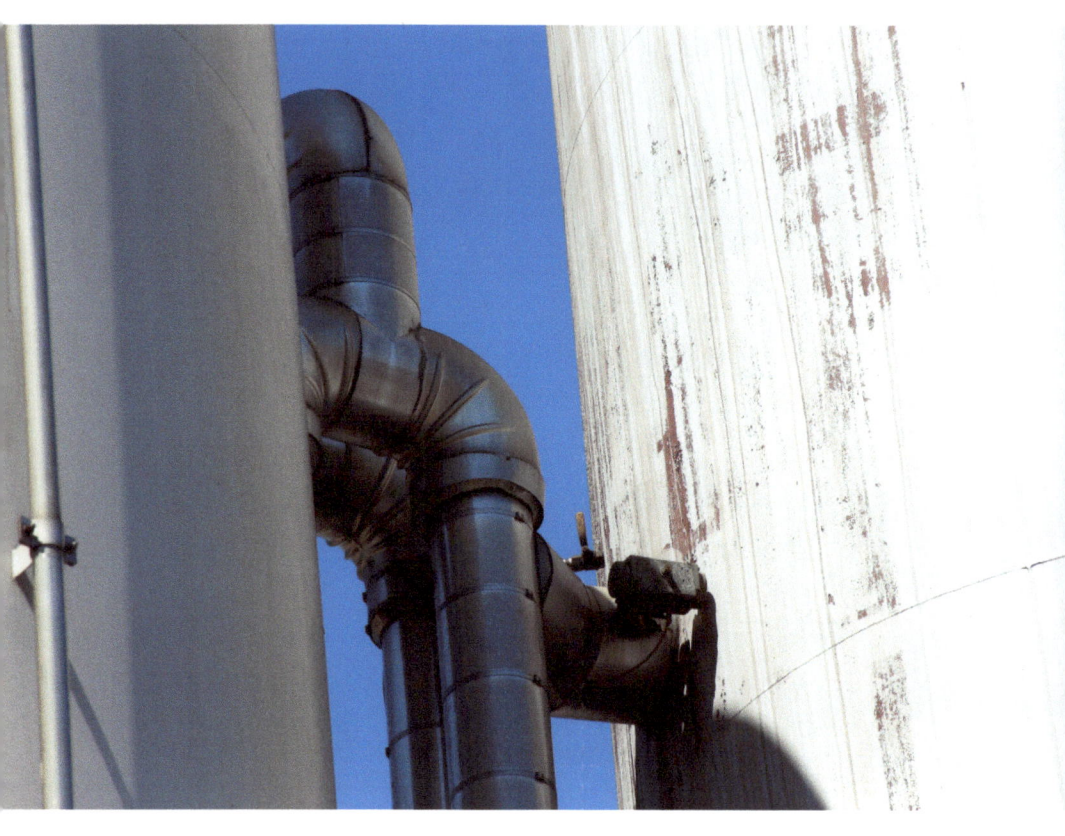

At lunch some of Aesop's classmates asked him for another story.

"But don't make it so complicated," said one.

"Right," said another. "And don't make us wait three days to hear how it ends."

The day before, Aesop had observed a pelican eating fish. He had made up a fable and had been practicing since then. He had been hoping for a chance to try it out.

"Okay," he said. "One beautiful day, a sea bream decided to swim closer to the surface to get a better view of the sun. The bream was just thinking what a great day it was when a pelican scooped it up for lunch."

He stopped and smiled. "That's it. Simple enough?"

"No!" said Gina. "What does *that* mean?"

Aesop looked at her. "Can't you figure it out?" He thought it was obvious.

She shook her head.

"No life lasts forever," Aesop said.

Most of his classmates thanked him politely and wandered off. It didn't seem like a very happy story.

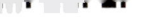

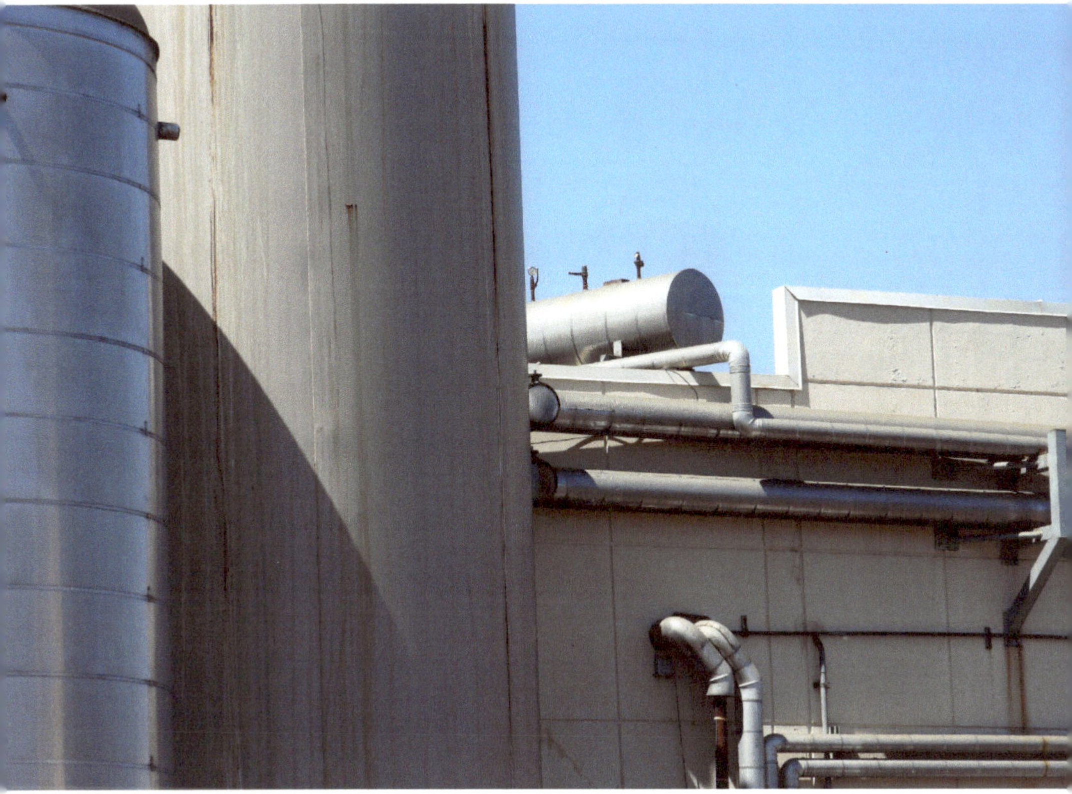

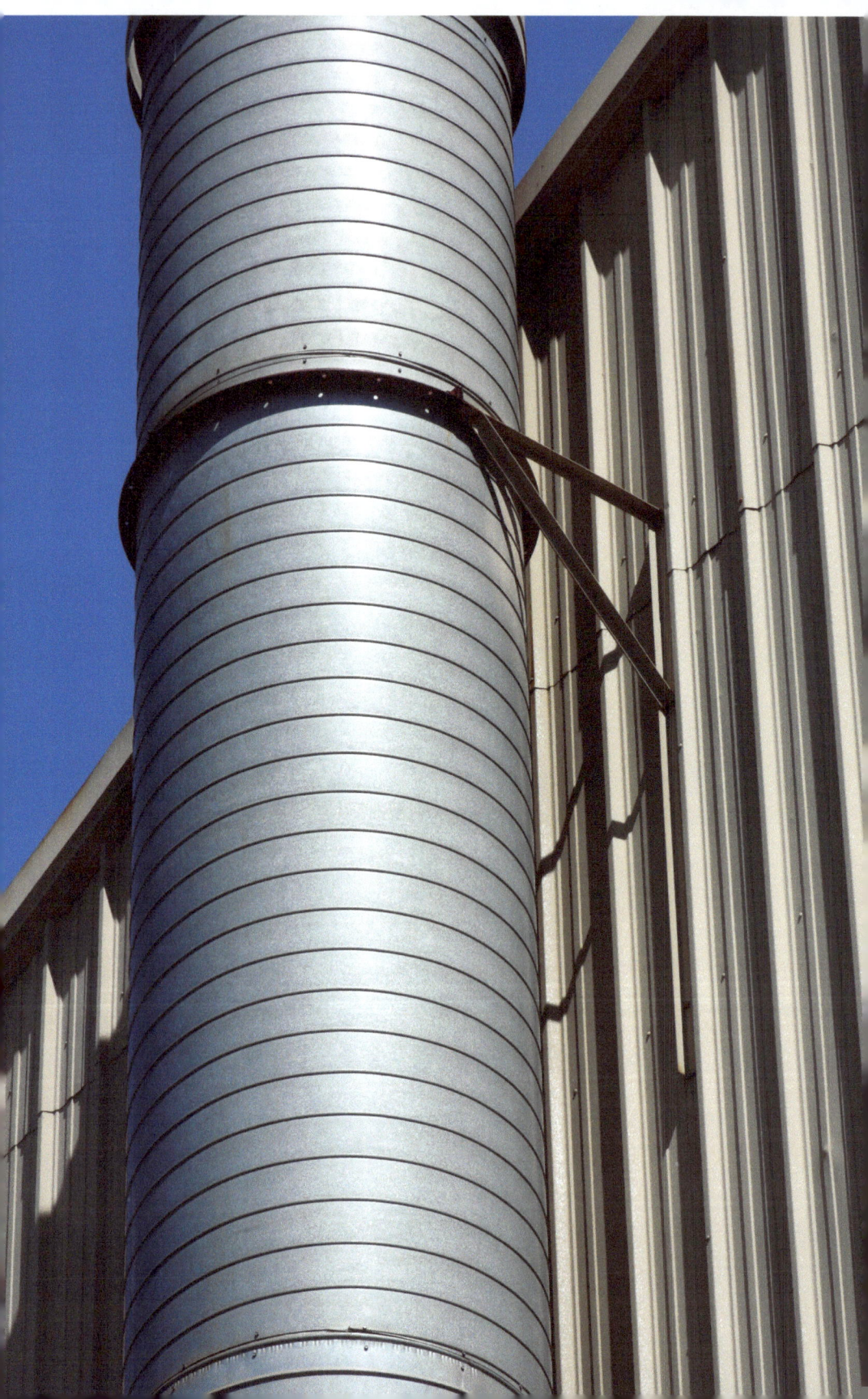

Tad hadn't been at school that day. When Tad's friends finally got a chance to look for him late in the afternoon, they found him not at home but in the swamp, looking for frogs.

"What are you *doing*?" Javan demanded. "We've been looking for you everywhere."

Tad shrugged. "When I first came down here I wanted see if I could get some luck," he said. "But once I started looking around, I kind of got lost. It's beautiful here."

"Beautiful," scoffed Javan. "Right. You *did* get lost. This is a *swamp*." Then he got to the point. "You can't stay here forever you know."

"I might," said Tad. "It seems safer."

Damian frowned. "The swamp is *not* safe," he said. His uncle had drowned in the swamp three winters earlier. "Besides, your dad's going to kill you if you don't go home."

Tad didn't reply. He thought it was probably the other way around: that his dad might kill him if he *did* go home. But he was glad to see his friends and started walking with them. After they walked a while he at last consented to go home.

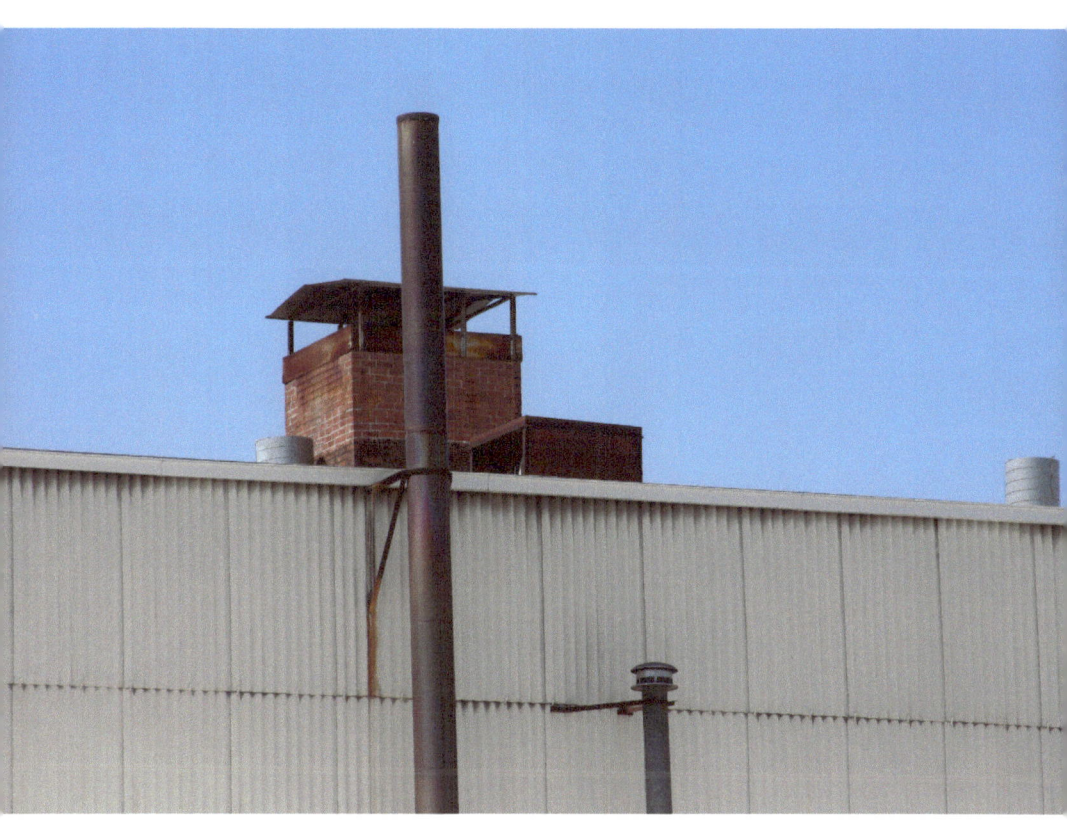

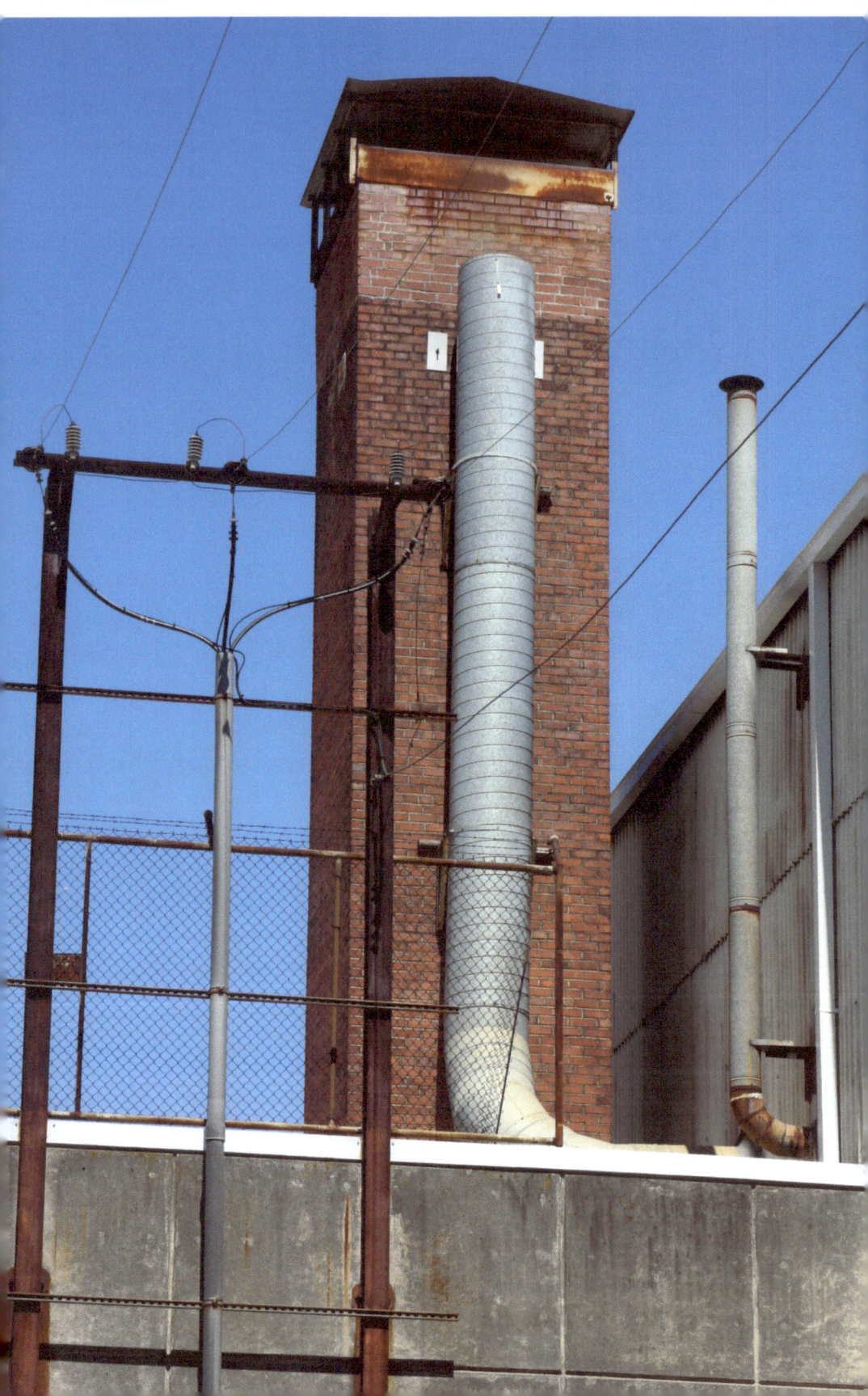

When they got to Tad's house, it was empty.

"I saw your dad at Pancho's," Damian said. "He'll be home soon."

Tad blanched. "Why didn't you *say* that? I should have stayed where I was."

"You can't stay in the swamp," Javan said.

"I could try."

A few minutes later, Javan and Damian left Tad and went to their own homes.

That evening Tad curled up in his bed, hoping he'd gotten enough luck from the frogs he had seen. He fell into a restless sleep.

His father stumbled home late and headed straight for Tad's bed. He shook Tad awake. *"Where* have you been?" he roared. "Don't *ever* leave home again." He clenched his fist and pulled back his arm to hit his son. Had he been sober, he was so mad he might have killed him. But the action threw him off balance and he fell backwards instead. He landed in a heap on the floor and started laughing. "I can't even hit a boy. I *must* be drunk." Within a few minutes he had fallen asleep on the floor, a few feet from Tad's bed.

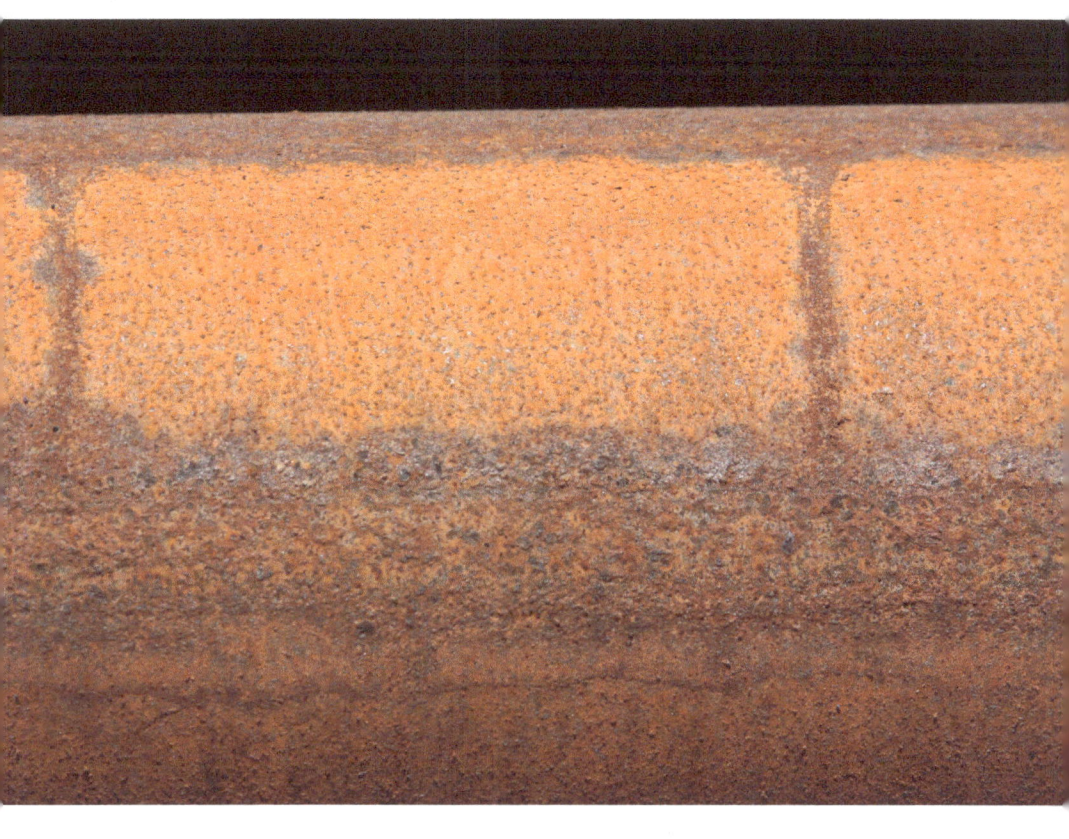

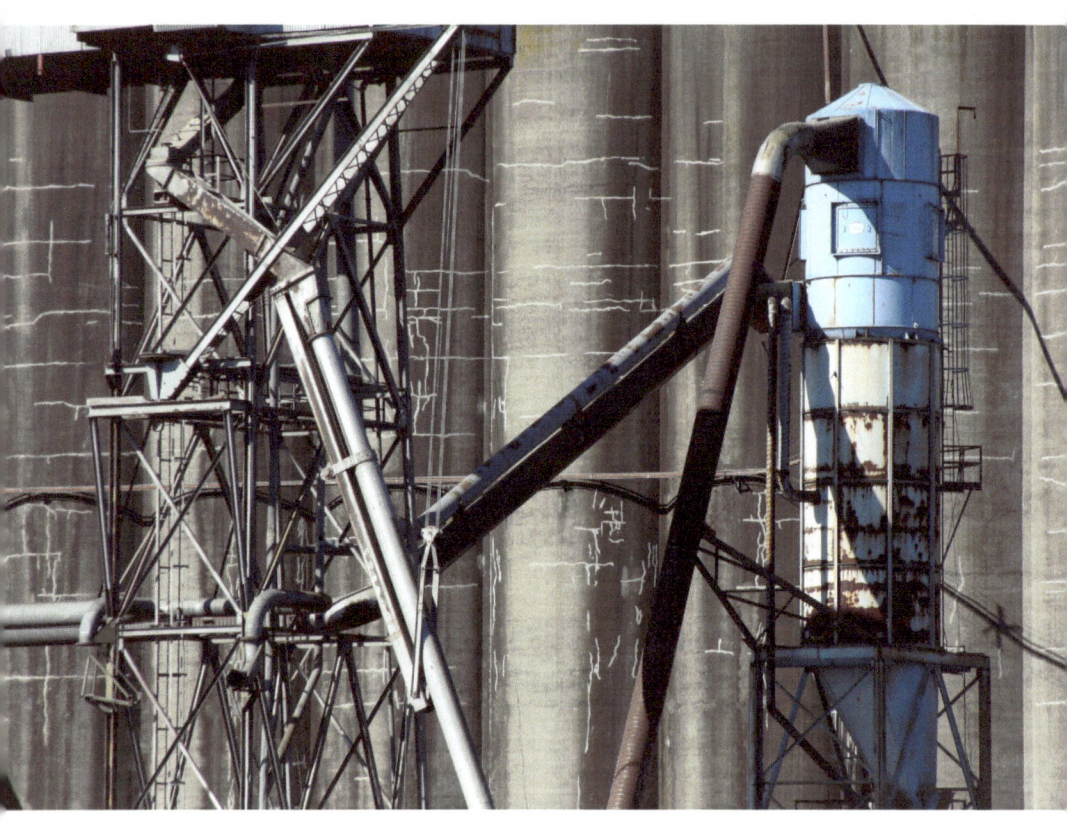

When his dad had been snoring for a few minutes, Tad got up as quietly as he could, packed a few clothes and all the scraps of food in the house, and slipped out the door. He headed straight for Aesop's.

The next morning Octavia found a boy curled up on the doorstep.

"Aesop," she called, "do you know who this is?"

Aesop came over and glanced down. His mouth set in a straight line. "It's Tad. Tad Garis."

"And why is he here?"

"I don't know," Aesop said.

But now Tad was awake. "Please," he said. "I want to stay with you."

Aesop's eyes widened but he didn't say anything. Only a week before Tad had been beating him up.

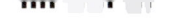

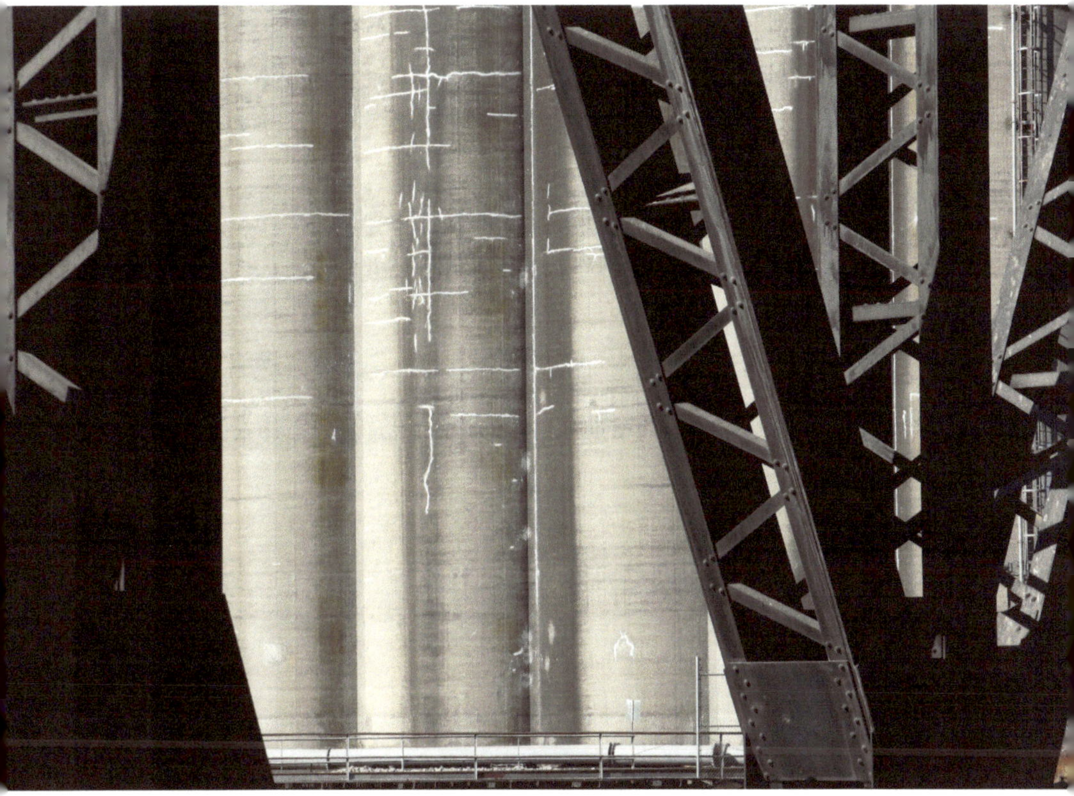

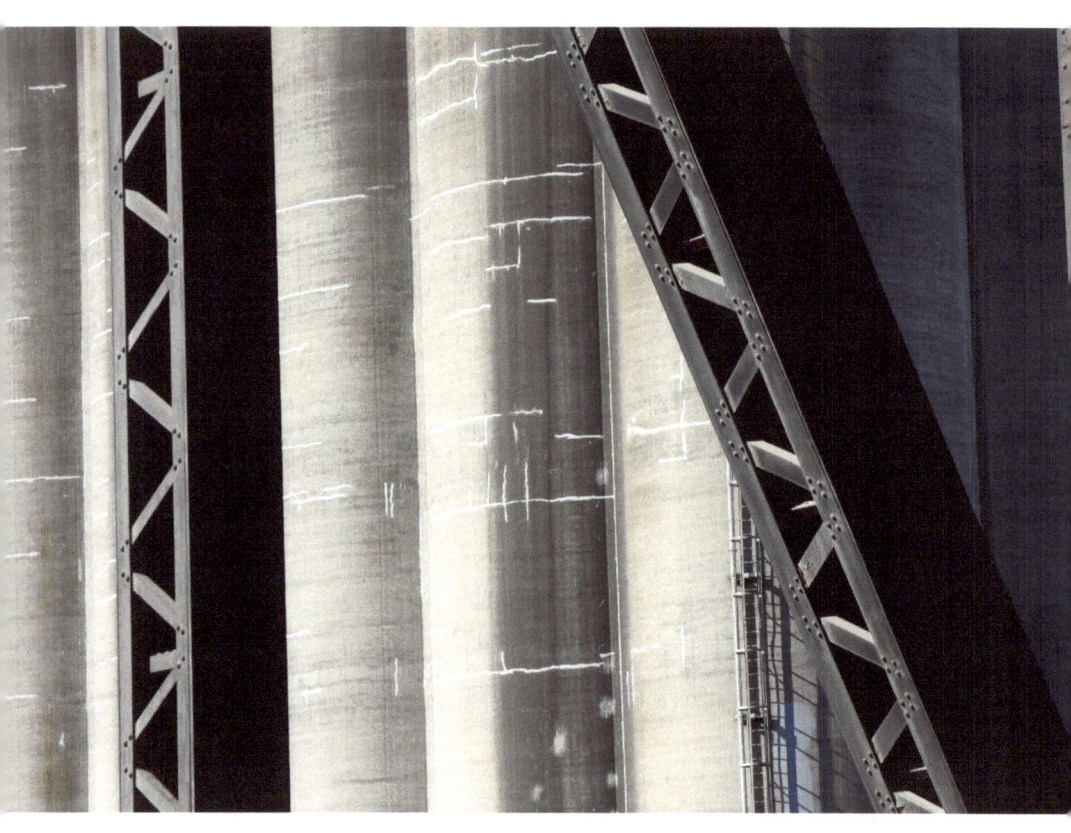

When Octavia heard the boy's last name, she had no trouble remembering his delivery, eleven years prior. His mother had died in childbirth. His father had been drinking and had thrown everyone out of the house. At the time, Octavia had wondered if the child would survive. She could guess what his home life had been like since then.

"Come in for breakfast," she said. "Let's talk." But neither boy said much during the meal, in spite of her attempts to coax them into conversation.

In the end, Octavia sent Tad to school without replying to his request. She wanted to know more details before she did anything. "Give us a couple days," she had told Tad. "Let us think about it."

Tad didn't answer. He wasn't going to risk staying at home any more. If he couldn't stay with Aesop, he was going to live at the swamp. He had found an abandoned shack, and he thought he could stay there.

When he left Octavia's, Tad headed for the shack instead of going to school. If he went to school, his dad might see him when he passed The Broken Wheel, and he didn't want that to happen.

A couple hours later, Javan found Aesop during a break at school. "If Tad gets into trouble at the swamp," Javan said, "it's going to be *your* fault."

Aesop said nothing. He had been thinking the same thing.

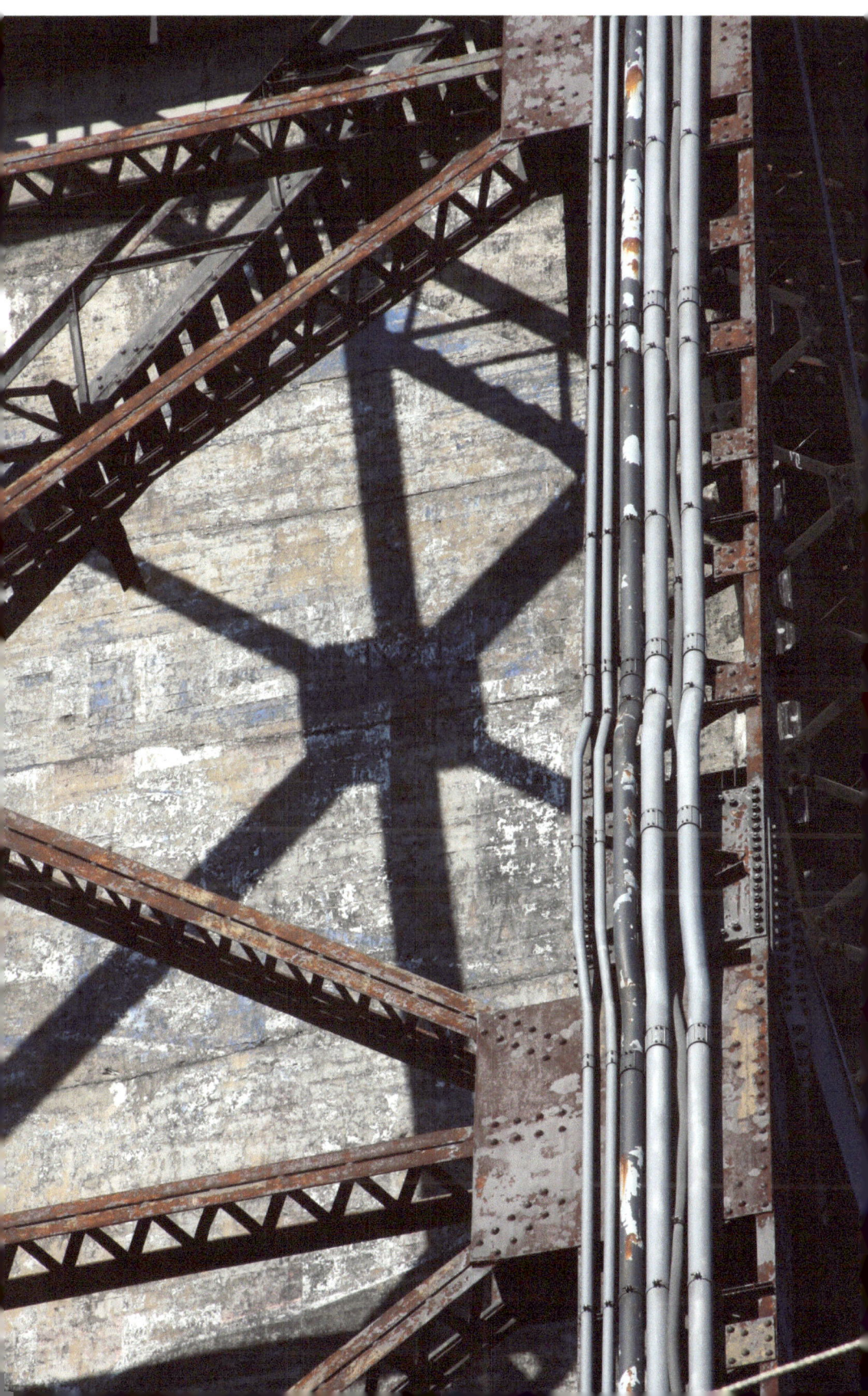

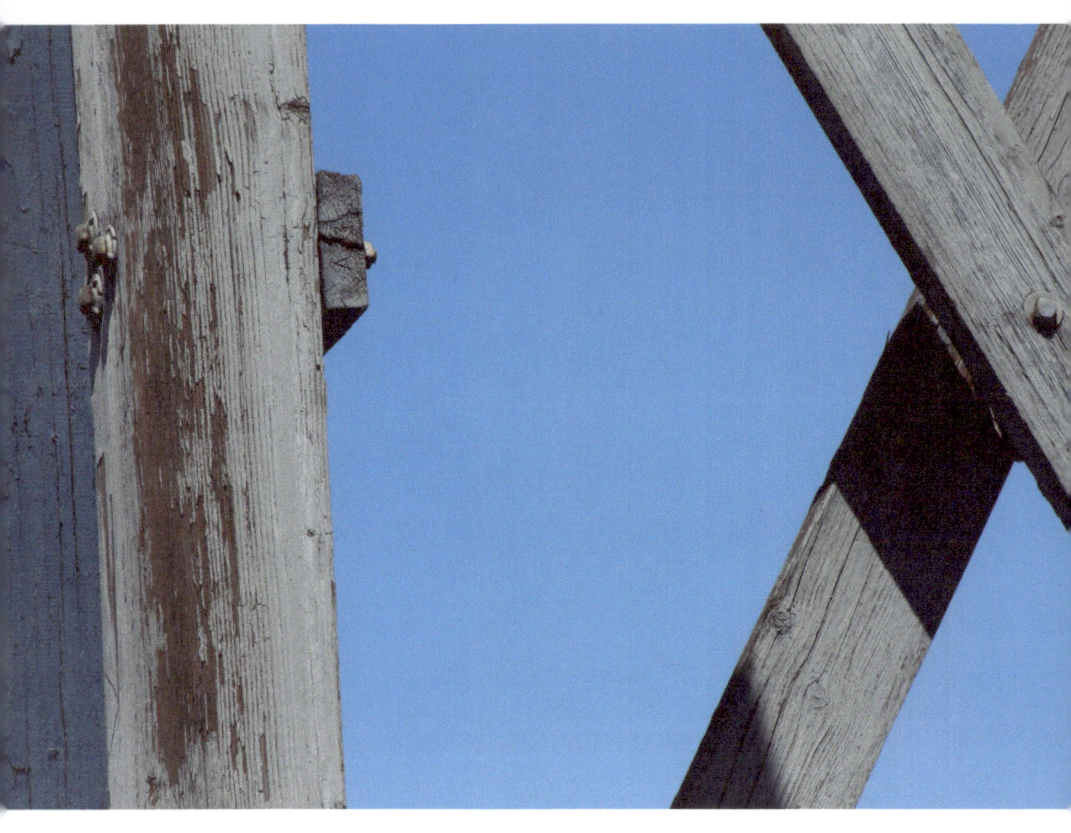

Tad wasn't at school the next two days. The third day, Octavia asked how Tad was doing. Aesop said he didn't know; that he hadn't been at school.

"Take him some food and go see how he is," Octavia demanded.

Aesop protested, but Octavia insisted.

When Aesop arrived at the swamp, he called for Tad. He got no response.

Aesop had thought he'd find Tad right away. But when Tad didn't answer, Aesop thought Tad might be hiding. Aesop searched for more than an hour. He found some footprints around Old Man Gregor's abandoned shack and tracks of some animals, but he couldn't find Tad. Finally he found a cap. Tad's cap. There was blood on it.

Aesop searched a few more minutes but he couldn't find anything else. Eventually he gave up and went to Tad's house. The house was deserted. Next he headed home.

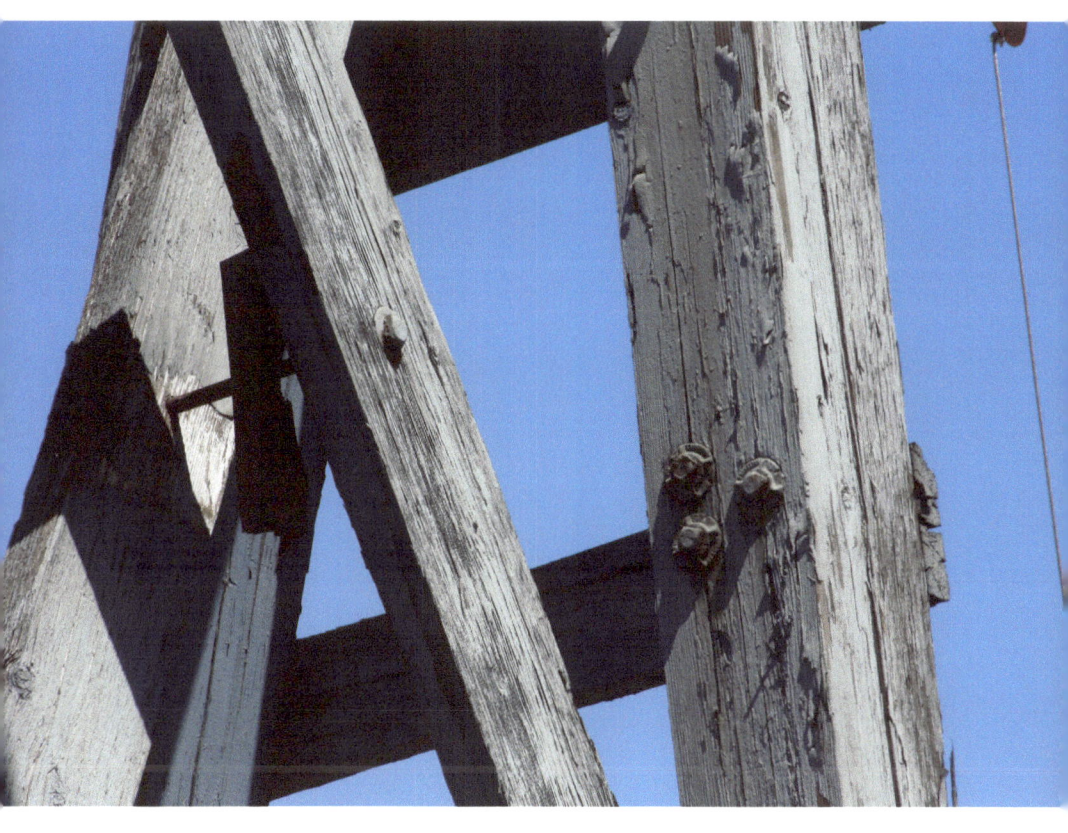

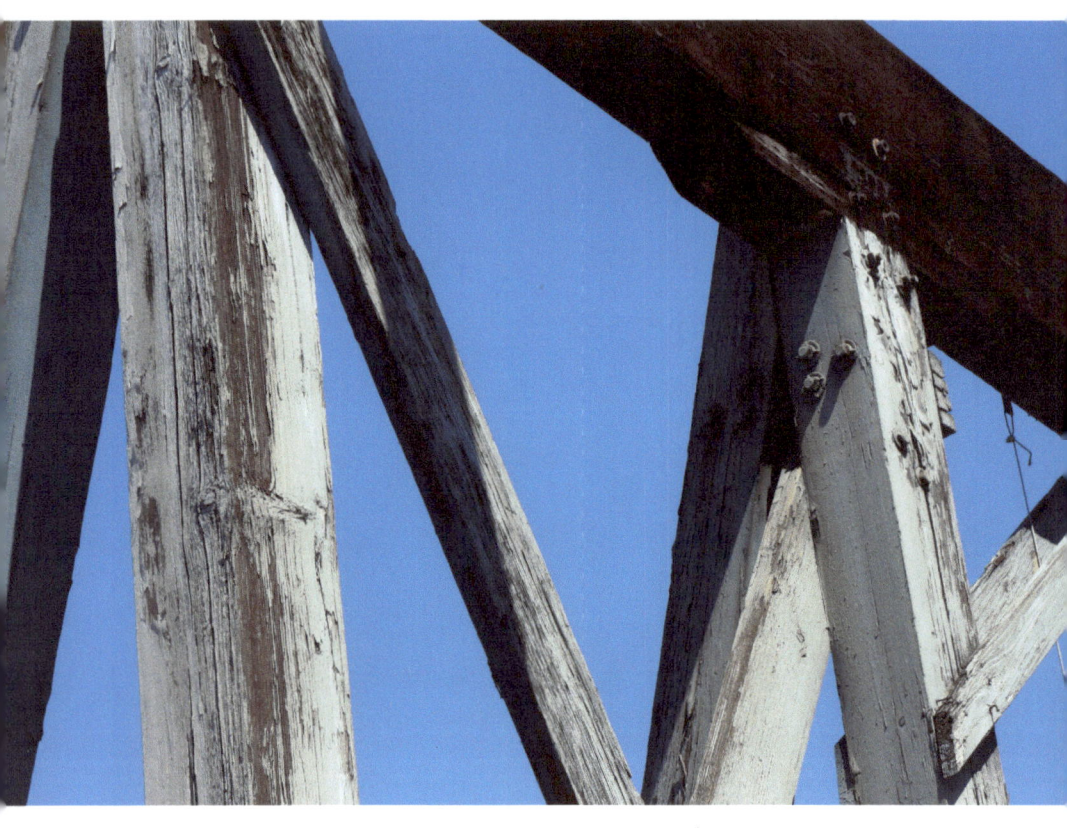

Octavia was just back from a delivery. "I could have used your help," she said. "*That* family needed some luck. Where were you?"

Aesop held up the cap.

"What's that?" she asked.

"It's Tad's cap. I found it in the swamp."

"What were you doing *there*?"

"You told me to find Tad."

"In the *swamp*?"

"I think it's where he lives now."

"Aesop. He lives at the swamp and you didn't tell me? Why doesn't he live at home?"

Aesop shrugged. He didn't want to say that it might be his fault.

But Octavia could guess why Tad might not be living at home.

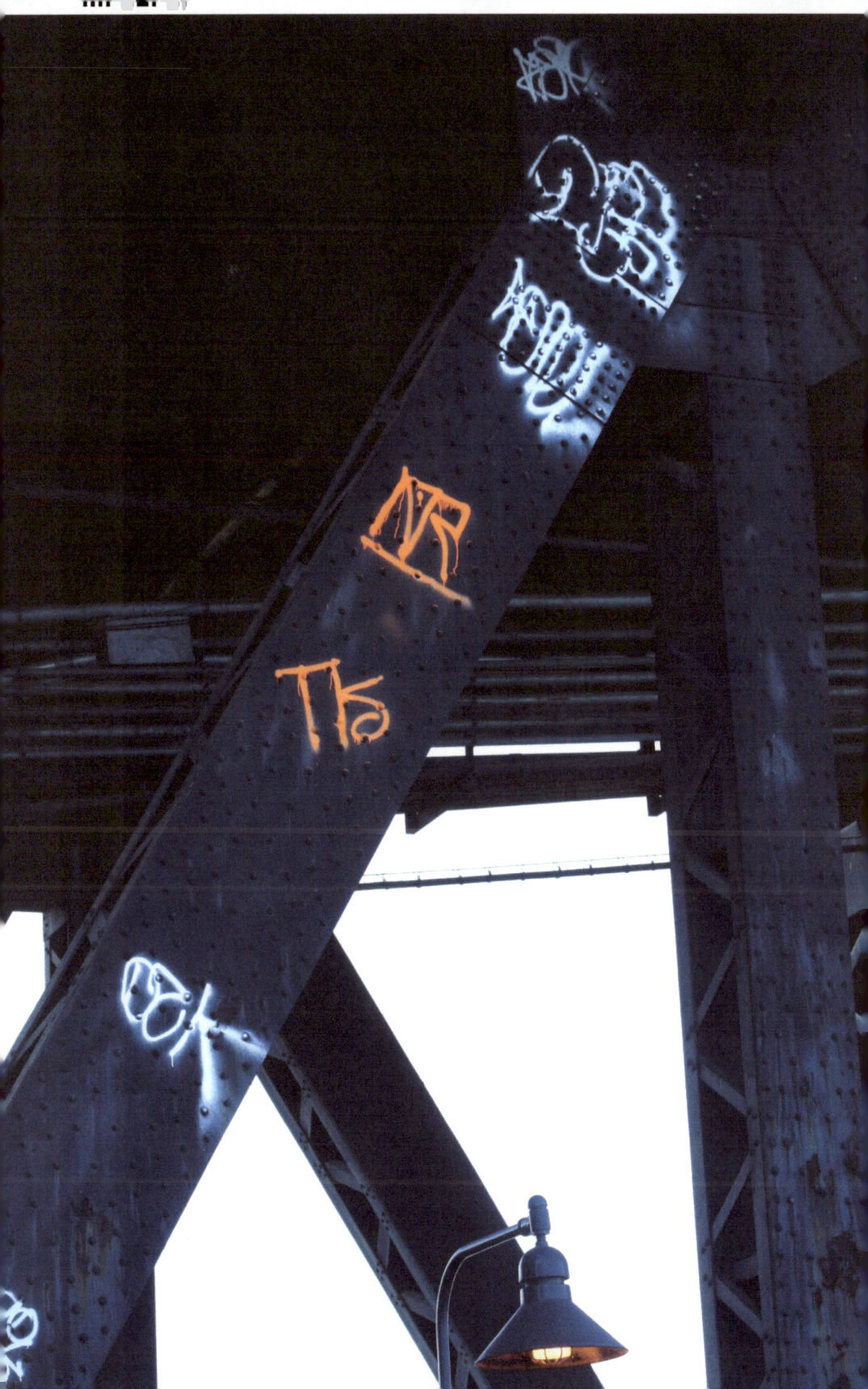

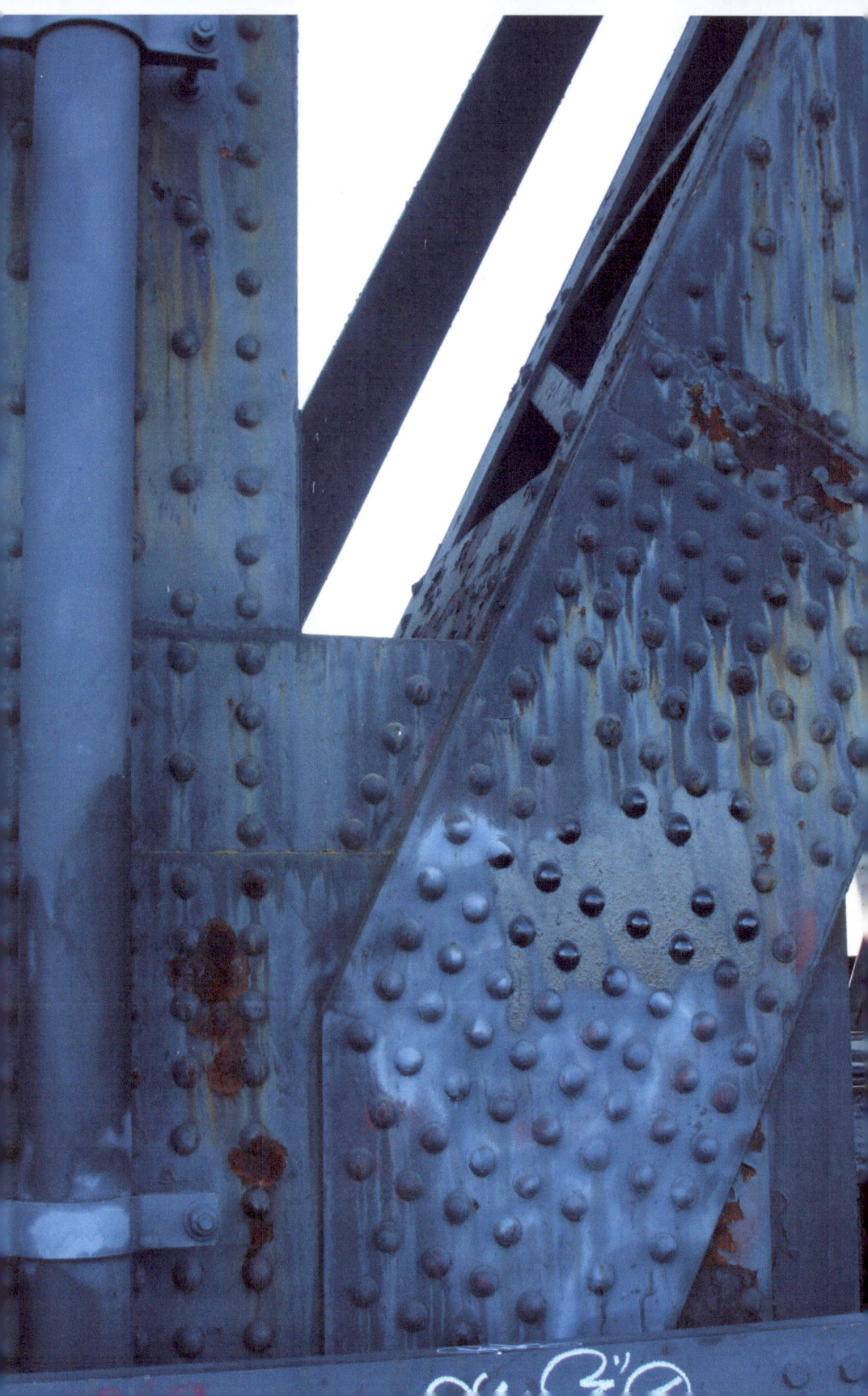

"When did you last see him?" Octavia asked.

"When he was here for breakfast."

"When he was *here*? Aesop, that was three days ago."

Then Octavia noticed the blood on the cap. She put on her jacket and handed Aesop his. "Okay," she said. "Come on. Bring the cap."

When they got to the town guards, Octavia told Aesop to tell them what he knew.

The guards knew Tad's father. They had been called to The Broken Wheel several times.

The guards rounded up a few citizens and a couple dogs and headed for the swamp. They only had an hour before sunset. As it turned out, they didn't need a lot of time because of the dogs.

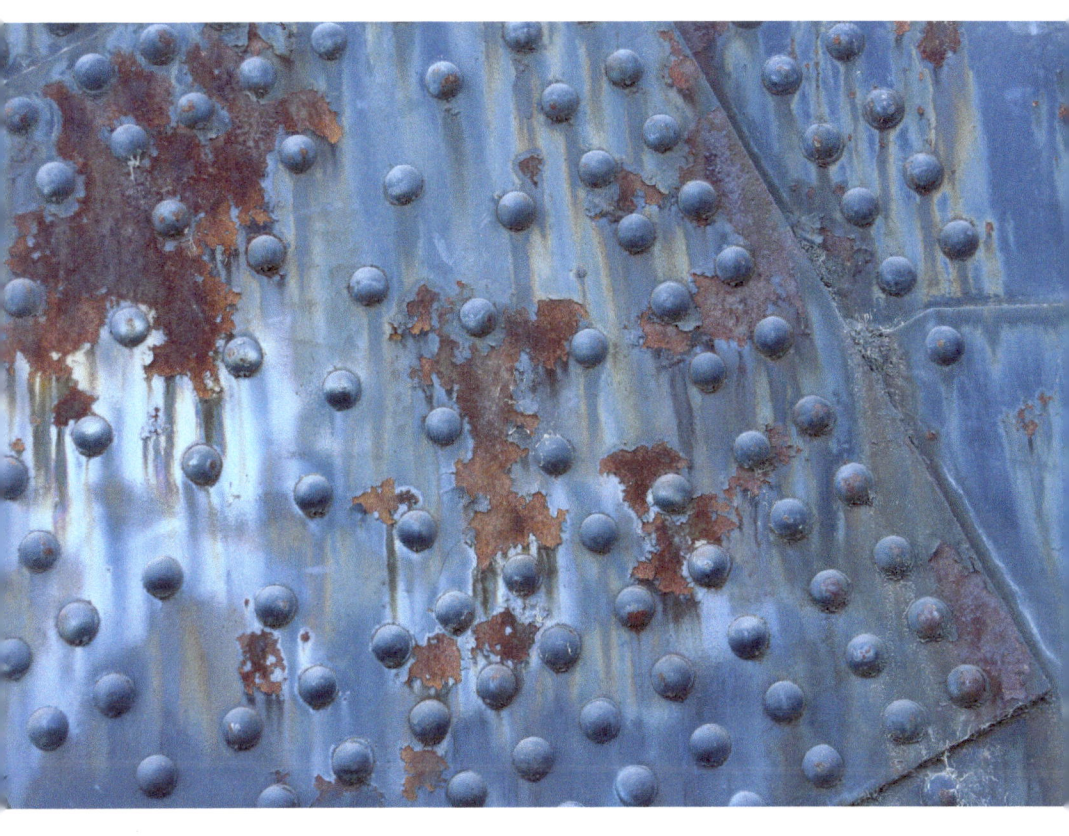

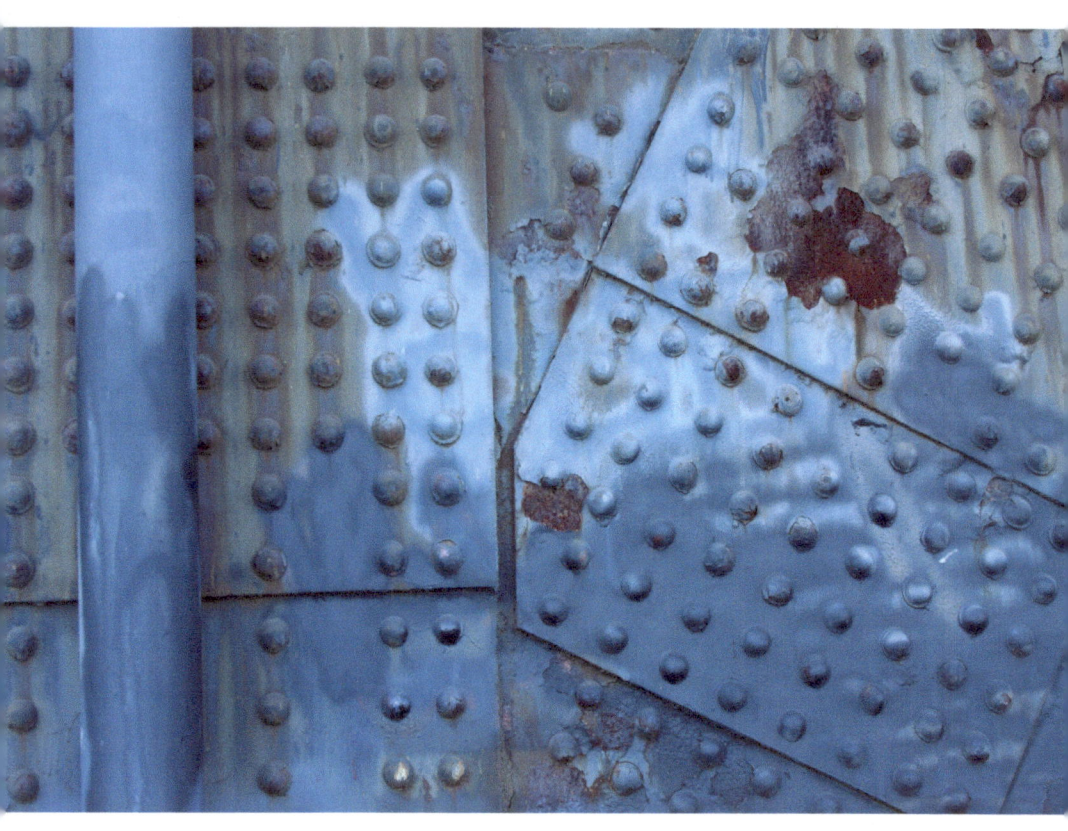

Tad's body was not in good shape. He had died a day or two before. He had on the same pants as when he'd had breakfast with Octavia and Aesop, but he had on a different shirt.

When the guards checked Tad's house they found no sign of life. They finally found Tad's father at The Broken Wheel.

"We're looking for your son," they said. "He hasn't been at school."

"He's down at the swamp."

"When was the last time you saw him?"

"Two days ago. He was in Old Man Gregor's abandoned shack. He'd ruined his shirt. Written some gibberish on it."

"Did you discipline him?"

"I might have hit him. He had ruined his shirt."

"Did you go back to check on him after that?"

"Why should I? He knows where the house is. When he's hungry he'll come home."

The guards looked at each other. "He's not coming home, Mr. Garis. We're placing you under arrest."

Hektor protested and tried to resist, but the guards overpowered him.

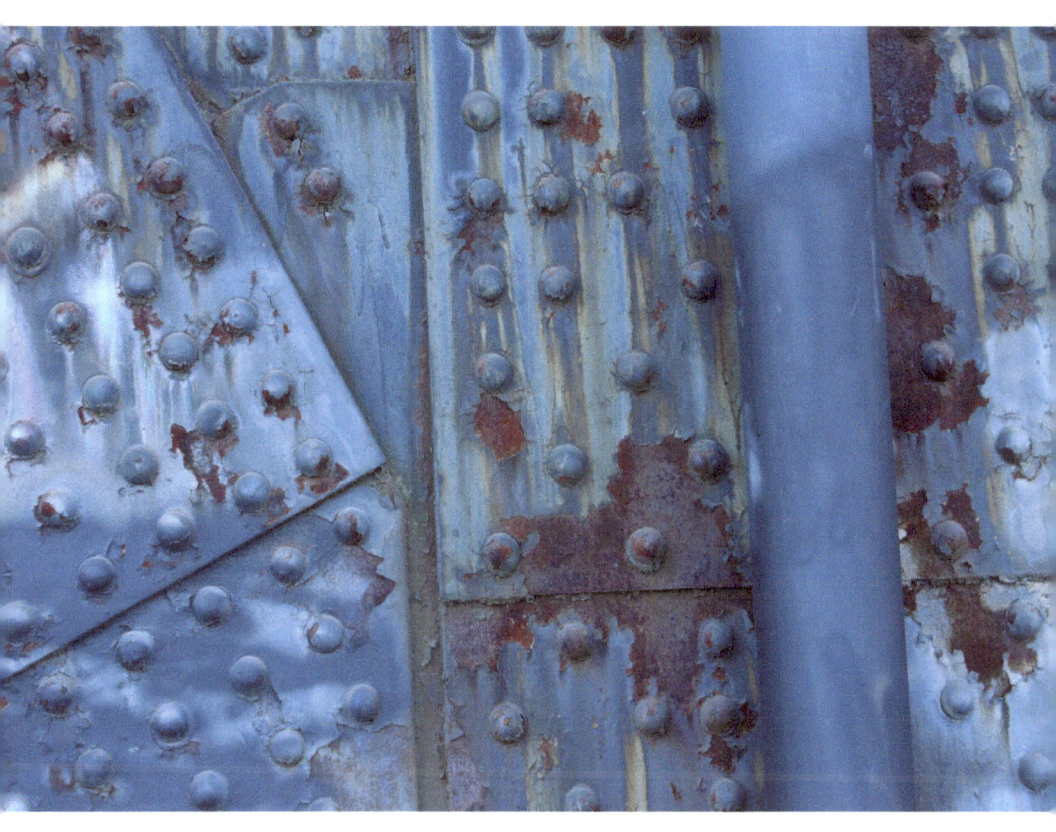

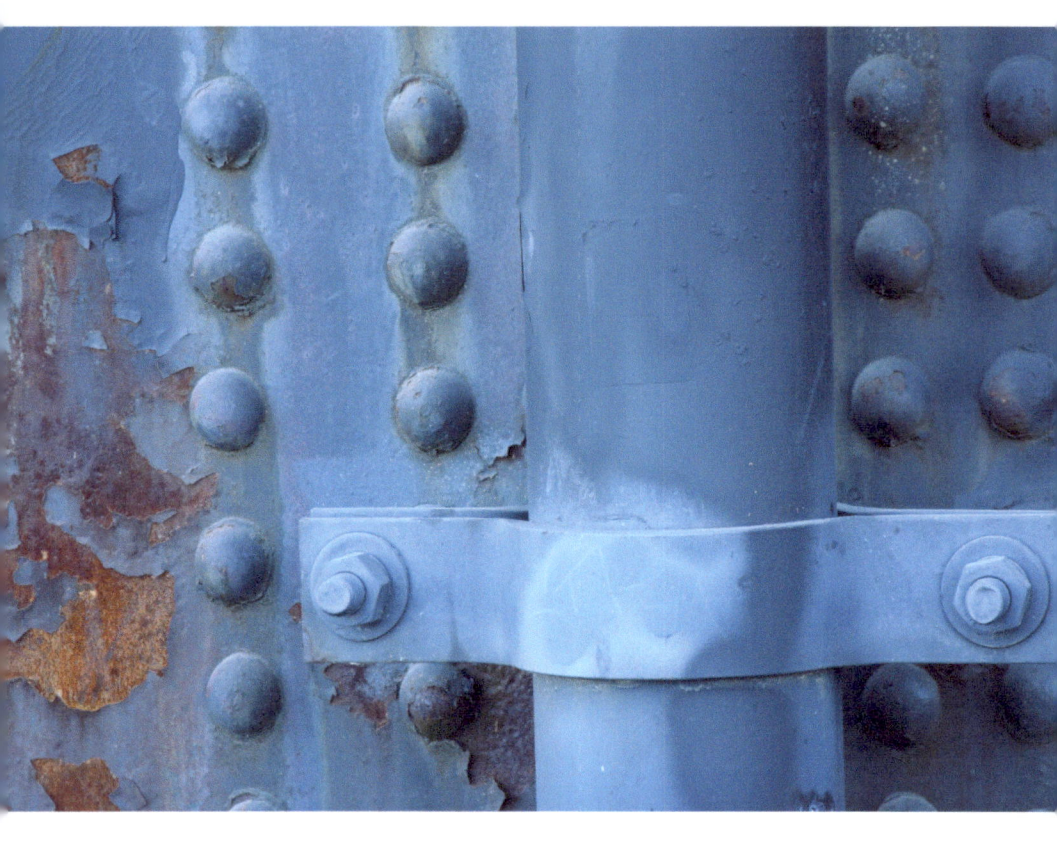

As news of Tad's death filtered through the town, several people wondered about things they had said and done.

Aesop was worried because he had told Tad he could be lucky if frogs saw him. Without hearing that, Tad never would have been at the swamp. He might still be alive.

Octavia had told Tad to wait, rather than inviting him to stay at her house while she sorted things out. If she'd invited him in, he might still be alive.

Damian had visited Tad at the swamp and told him Aesop's riddle about the rooster. When he'd left, Damian had met Hektor, who had demanded to know where Tad was. Damian had told him. Now Damian was thinking if he hadn't said anything, his friend might still be alive.

Others had similar thoughts, including Jurek, one of the guards, who had wondered about Tad's home life only a month before when he had arrested Tad's father for brawling. But other than arresting Hektor, he had done nothing.

And, sitting in jail, Hektor learned he had hit Tad on the head a few hours before he died. As Hektor gradually sobered up, he realized he might be in trouble just because he had tried to knock some sense into his worthless son.

"I think it's my fault," Aesop told Octavia. They had gone down to Gregor's cabin to talk and to grieve.

"Come here," Octavia said. She was sitting on the rickety stoop, her legs dangling. She hugged her son as he sat beside her.

"You need to do your best," she said. "But you aren't responsible for what other people do. Just do your best and learn from your mistakes." She paused.

"We all make mistakes," she said. "Maybe I should have let Tad stay with us when he asked. Right now, I'm sorry I didn't. But we don't know what would have happened. Maybe his dad would have come and hurt us all. You don't know what would have happened. Do your best. It's all you can do."

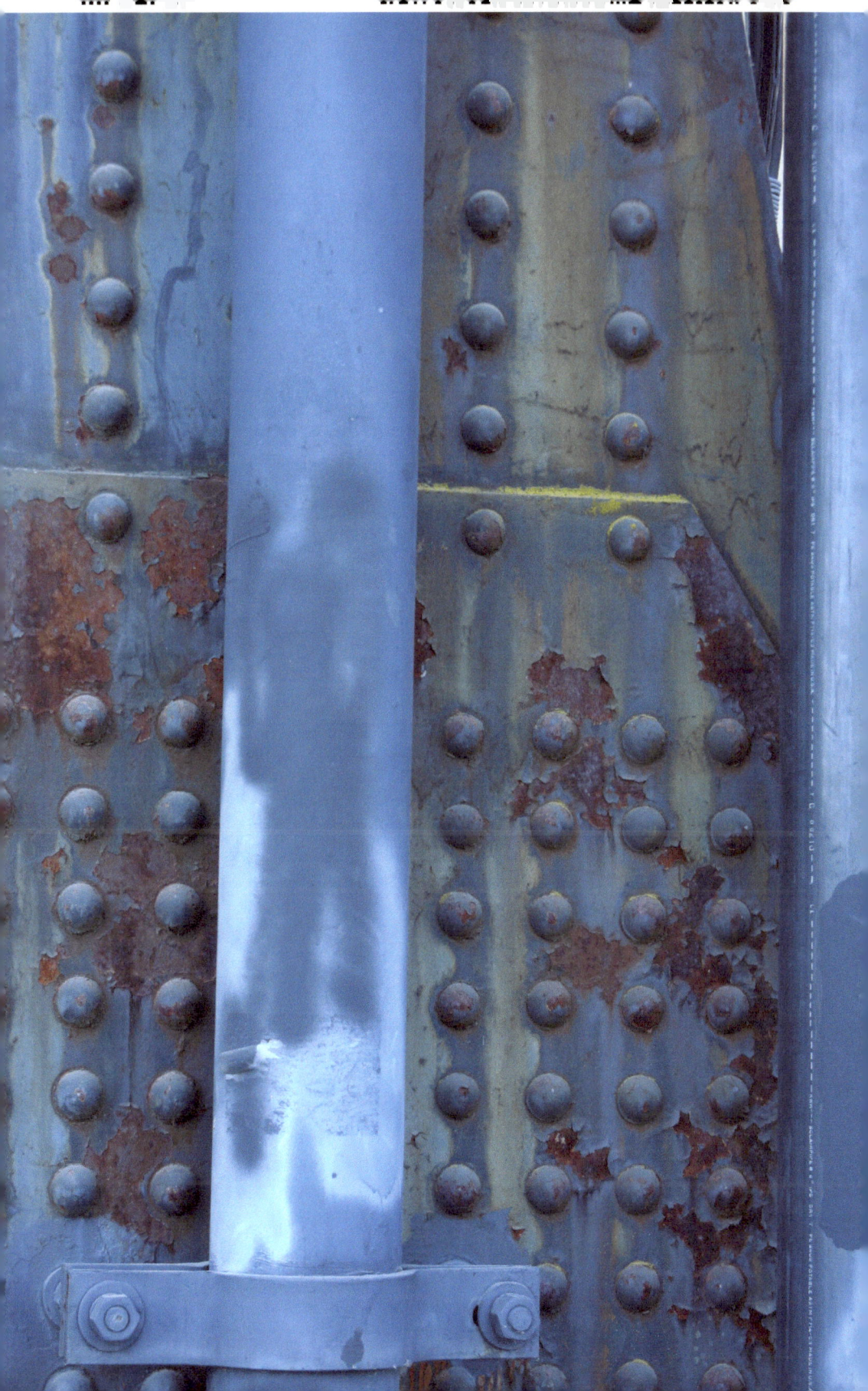

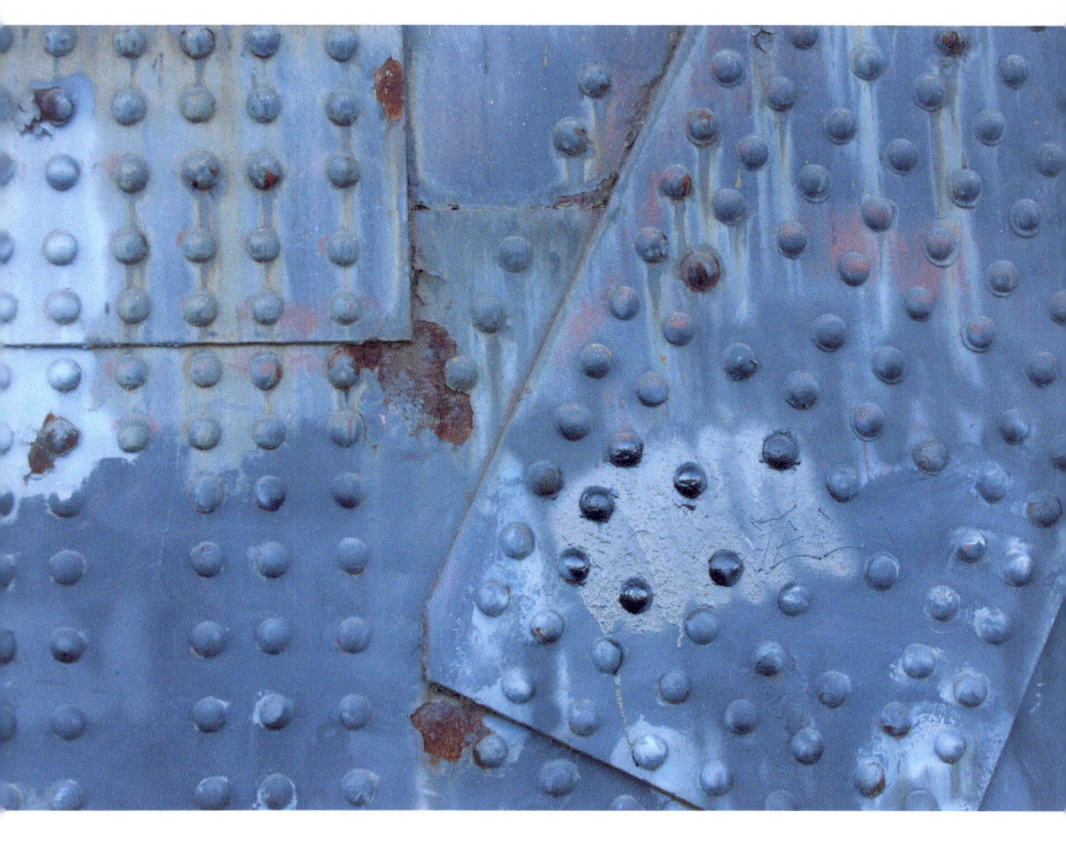

"Tad was starting to like the swamp," Aesop said. "He could have learned a lot here."

Octavia was silent. She knew her son had learned a lot by hiking and observing nature. She had no doubt that Tad likewise could have benefited by observing life at the swamp.

"I'm sorry, Aesop," she said, holding him close.

When she looked down at her son, she noticed a gap between the wooden slats of the stoop, a little to his left. The gap allowed her to see some fabric on the ground below. Octavia let go of Aesop and reached down to pick it up. It was the shirt Tad had been wearing when he had visited three days earlier and had asked to stay at her house. It had quite a bit of blood on the back. She turned it over. She gasped. In big charcoal letters on the front it said, "I'm with Aesop."

"Oh Aesop," she said. "This might not get any easier."

It's like the sea bream, Aesop thought glumly. No life lasts forever. But some end before we're ready.

~~

Reflection questions

What do you think about Tad moving to the swamp? Was that a bad move? A good move? Or something in between?

Could anyone have made a difference for Tad?

How about the boys and girls like Tad in *your* city. Could anyone make a difference for them?

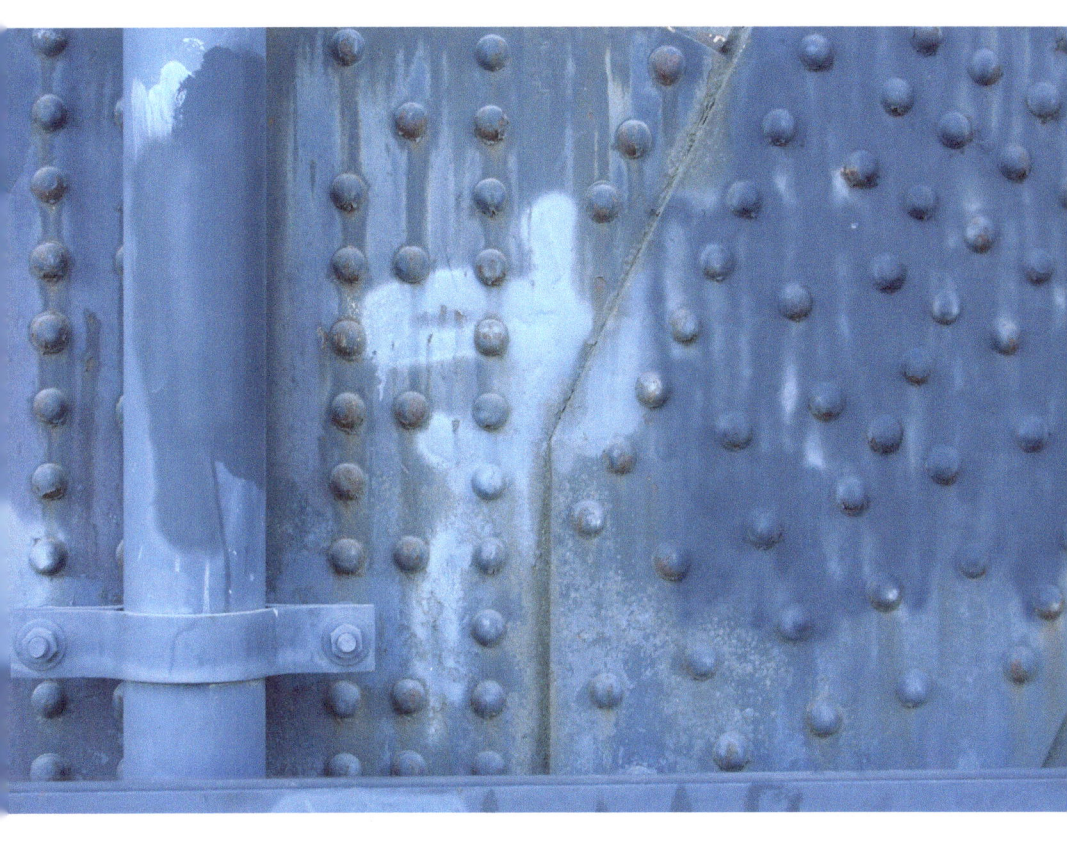

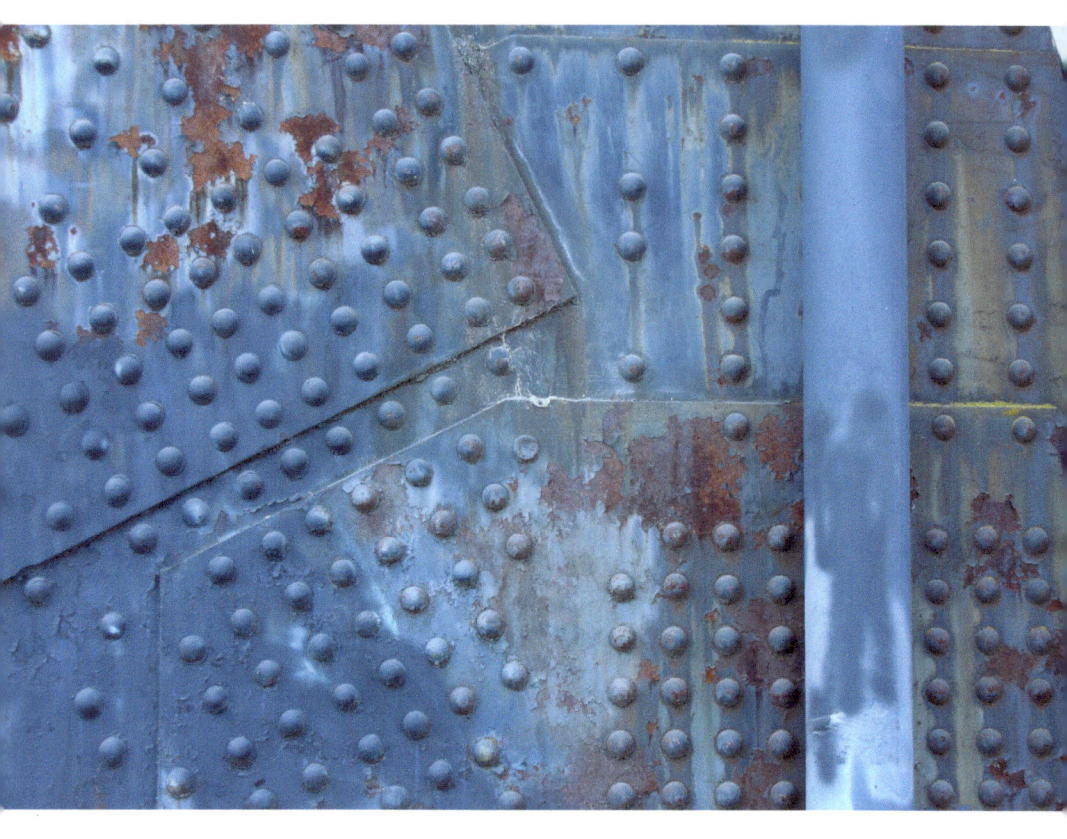

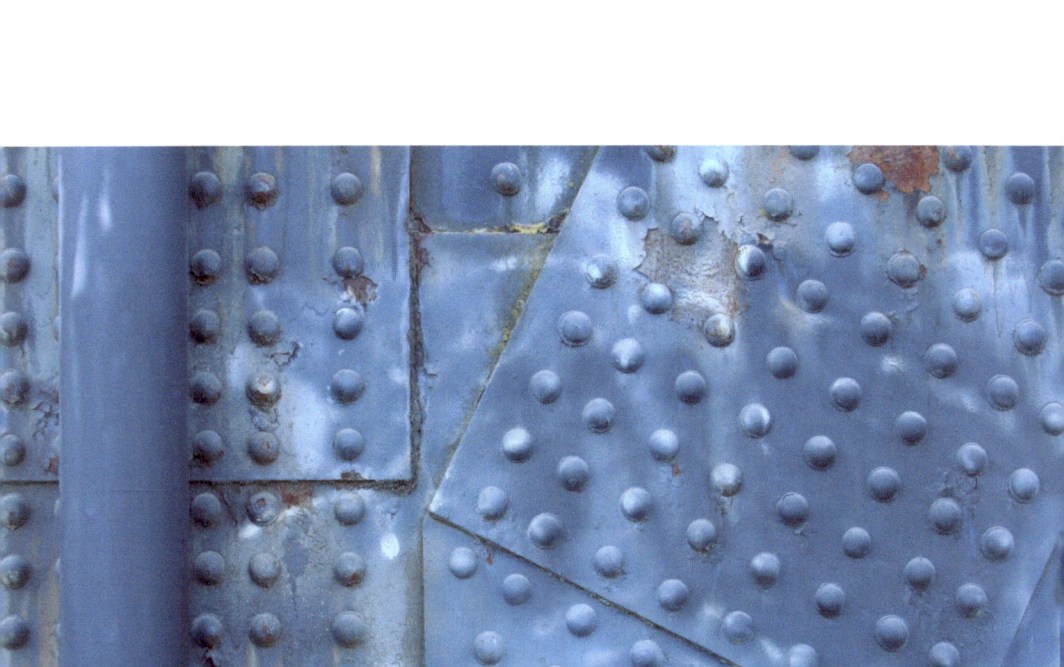

A Mark Dahle Portfolio

Tad And The Frogs

Friends Can Be Found In Unusual Places

(Fables About Aesop #5)

This Mark Dahle Portfolio includes a colorful painting, twenty-five beautiful photographs from Freiburg, Germany and Hawaii, and a story about Aesop making some unusual friends.

Octavia held Tad's shirt. Tad had written "I'm with Aesop" in big letters on the front.

"What does *that* mean?" she asked.

This Mark Dahle Portfolio includes a colorful painting, twenty-six beautiful photographs from Detroit, and a story about a carpenter who made fine furniture from scraps.

The carpenter came across the twig one day while scouring the countryside for debris. He had already found a sheet of plastic, a broken piece of plywood and several rusty, bent nails. Those he knew he could use. But the twig? He could not imagine a use for it. Nevertheless, it caught his attention as he walked along the edge of a forest. He absentmindedly picked it up.

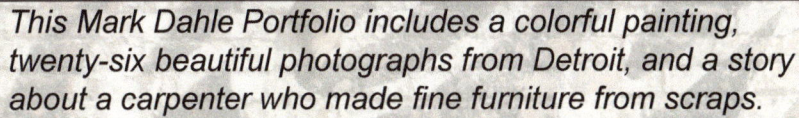

A Mark Dahle Portfolio

The Carpenter And The Twig

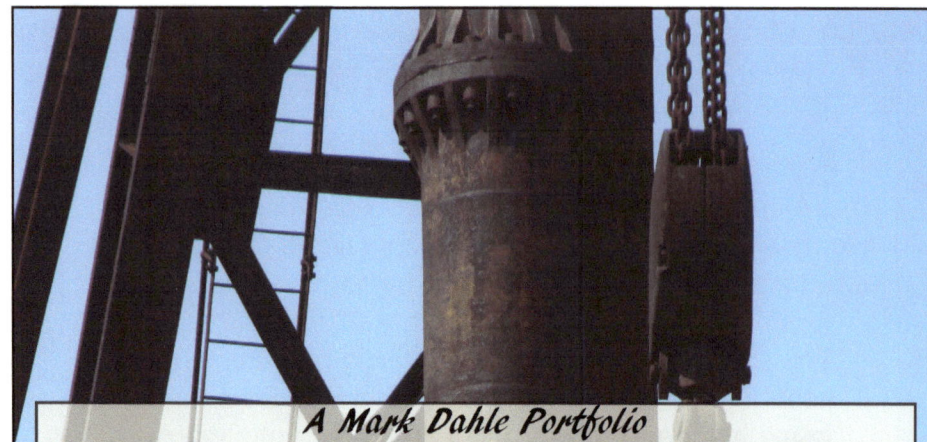

A Mark Dahle Portfolio

The Eighth Anniversary Of LuniGrab

Terminal Three #1

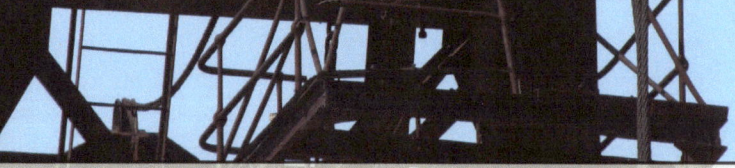

This Mark Dahle Portfolio includes a colorful abstract painting, twenty-five beautiful photographs from Venice, Italy, and the first story about a member of the resistance on a mission to Whitehorse.

Everyone expected trouble today, and to be arriving at the crowded airport on such an anniversary felt like madness.